The Value of Offshore Banking
to the Global Financial System

The Value Of Offshore Banking To The Global Financial System

JOHN BAIDEN, B.Sc., MBA, M.Sc.
(distinction), JD, LL.M (distinction)
Central University College

Library of Congress Control Number:		2011915513
ISBN:	Hardcover	978-1-4653-5924-7
	Softcover	978-1-4653-5923-0
	Ebook	978-1-4653-5925-4

To order additional copies of this book, contact:
Xlibris Corporation
1-888-795-4274
www.Xlibris.com
Orders@Xlibris.com
104426

CONTENTS

INTRODUCTION

The global financial system is the collection of markets, institution, laws, regulations and techniques though which bonds, stocks and other securities are traded, interest rates are determined and financial services including payments are produced and delivered around the world. The global financial system is seen to serve seven vital functions namely, Savings, Wealth, Liquidity, Credit, Payment, Risk Protection and Policy Functions.[1]

An offshore Bank is a bank located outside the Country of residence of depositor, usually offering low taxes and bank secrecy to provide the depositor with financial and legal advantages.[2] Offshore banks predominate in offshore Financial Centers (OFCs). Other financial services in the OFC's are insurance and securities.[3] An offshore bank may however be "full service", meaning offering other financial

---

[1] Frederic S. Mishkin and Stanley Eakins, *"Financial Markets and Institutions"*, 4th Edition, 2003 (Addison Wesley).
[2] Salim M. Darbs, R. Barry Johnston, and Mary G. Zephrin, "Filling a gap in global surveillance", Finance and Development September 2003, p.34.
[3] id

services incidental to banking such as trading in securities, investment advisory, underwriting etc. Also to be found in offshore financial centers are non-financial activities like shipping registry.[4]

A jurisdiction is considered an offshore financial center if its financial sector accounts for a significant and disproportionate share of its domestic economy. [5]

Offshore Banks are conditioned upon jurisdictions that are more 'hospitable' or have incentives to cause their existence. Some of the conditions are no or low taxes, lax or less stringent banking regulations, and better privacy, laws. These jurisdictions are typically known as 'Tax Havens'. One cannot understand offshore banking without understanding 'Tax Havens'. Tax havens are in effect designed to be off shore financial centers of which Banks usually predominate.

This paper intends to examine the causes of offshore banking and its advantages and disadvantages to determine whether it has any 'value 'or 'utility' to the global financial system and how it impacts on our 'economic welfare, civil liberties and standard of living'. The paper will finally conclude on the issue of whether the present global movements towards the closure of Tax havens have any merit or 'currency'.

---

[4]   id
[5]   id

THE GLOBAL FINANCIAL SYSTEM

The global financial system is the collection of markets, institutions, laws, regulations and techniques through which bonds, stocks, and other securities are traded, interest rates are determined and financial services including payments are produced and delivered around the world.[6]

The great importance of the financial system in our daily lives can be appreciated by reviewing the functions that it performs. The global financial system has seven basic functions that create a need for money and capital markets.[7]

SAVINGS FUNCTION

The global system of financial markets and institutions provides a conduit for the public's savings. Bonds, Stocks, and other financial claims sold in the money and capital markets provide a profitable, relatively low-risk outlet for the public's savings, which flow through the financial markets into

---

[6] Frederic S. Mishkin and Stanley Eakins, *"Financial Markets and Institutions"*, 4th Edition, 2003 (Addison Wesley).

[7] Peter Rose and Milton Marquis, "Money and Capital Markets", 10th Edition, 2008, (McGraw Hill)

investment so that more goods and services can be produced (i.e., productivity will rise), increasing the world's standard of living. When savings decline, investment and living standards begin to fall in those nations where savings are in short supply.[8]

WEALTH FUNCTION

While current savings represent a flow of funds, accumulated savings built up over time represent a stock of assets that we often refer to as wealth.[9] For those businesses and individuals choosing to save, the financial instruments sold in the money and capital markets provide an excellent way to store wealth (i.e. preserve the value of assets we hold) until funds are needed for spending. Although we might choose to store our wealth in "things" (e.g., automobiles), such items are subject to depreciation and often carry great risk of loss. However, bonds, stocks, and other financial instruments do not wear out over time and usually generate income, moreover, their risk of loss often is much less than for many other forms of stored wealth.[10]

LIQUIDITY FUNCTION

For wealth stored in financial instruments, the global financial marketplace provides a means of converting those

---

[8]   id

[9]   Peter Rose and Milton Marquis, "Money and Capital Markets", 10th Edition, 2008, (McGraw Hill)

[10]   id

instruments into cash with little risk of loss. The world's financial markets provide liquidity (immediate spendable cash) for savers who hold financial instruments but are in need of money. In modern societies, money consists mainly of currency and deposits held in banks, credit unions, and other depository institutions and are the only financial instrument possessing perfect liquidity. Money can be spent as it is without the necessity of converting it into some other form. However, money generally earns the lowest rate of return of all assets traded in the financial system, and its purchasing power is seriously eroded by inflation. That is why savers generally minimize their holdings of money and hold other, higher-yielding financial instruments until they really need spendable funds. Of course, money is not the only means of making purchase of goods and services.[11]

CREDIT FUNCTION

In addition to providing liquidity and facilitating the flow of savings into investment to build wealth, the global financial markets furnish credit to finance consumption and investment spending. Credit consists of a loan of funds in return for a promise of future payment.[12] Consumers need credit to purchase a home, buy groceries, repair the family automobile, and retire outstanding debts. Businesses draw on their lines of credit to stocks their shelves with inventory, construct new buildings, meet payrolls, and grant dividends

---

[11]   Peter Rose and Milton Marquis, "Money and Capital Markets", 10th Edition, 2008, (McGraw Hill)

[12]   id

to their stockholders. States, local, and federal government borrow to construct buildings and other public facilities and to cover cash expenses until tax revenues flow in.[13]

PAYMENT FUNCTION

The global financial system continuously provides instruments and other mechanism for making payments for goods and services across the globe.[14] Instruments like checks, cash, money orders, banker's drafts, letters of credit, credit cards, debit cards etc are innovations of the global financial system.[15] The financial system also offers mechanism like telegraphic transfers (e.g. SWIFT, Western Union, Money Gram etc.,), and other payment mediums like Automated Clearing House (ACH), Federal Wire, CHIPS. etc., which facilitates global trade and commerce.

RISK PROTECTION FUNCTION

The financial markets offer businesses, consumers, and governments' protection against life, health, property, and income risks. This is accomplished, first of all, by the sale of insurance polices.[16] Policies marketed by life insurance companies indemnify a family against possible loss of income following the death of a loved one. Property casualty insurers protect their policyholders against an incredibly wide array

---

[13] id

[14] id

[15] Peter Rose and Milton Marquis, "Money and Capital Markets", 10th Edition, 2008, (McGraw Hill)

[16] id

---

of personal and property risk, ranging from ill health and storm damage to negligence on the highways. In addition to making possible for sale of insurance policies, the money and capital markets have been used by businesses and consumers to "self-insure" against risk; that is, holdings of wealth are built up as protection against future losses. [17]

The financial system permits individuals and institutions to engage in both risk sharing and risk reduction. Risk sharing occurs when an individual or institution transfers risk exposure to someone willing to accept that risk (such as an insurance company), while risk reduction usually takes place when we diversify our wealth across a wide variety of different assets so that out overall losses are likely to be more limited.[18]

POLICY FUNCTION

Commercial Banks have been the principal channel through which government have carried out its policy of attempting to stabilize the economy and avoid inflation.[19] By manipulating interest rates and the availability of credit, government can affect the borrowing and spending plans of the public, impacting the growth of jobs, production, and prices. This task of economic stabilization has been given largely to central banks, such as the Federal Reserve System in the United States, the Bank of England, the Bank of Japan, and the new European Central Bank (the ECB).[20]

---

[17]   id
[18]   id
[19]   Peter Rose and Milton Marquis, "Money and Capital Markets", 10th Edition, 2008, (McGraw Hill)
[20]   id

OFFSHORE BANKING

What is it and where it is done?

Offshore banking is the cross-border intermediation of funds and provision of services by banks residing in offshore financial centers (OFCs) to nonresidents. [21]

Typically, offshore banks deal almost always with other financial institutions and transact wholesale business dominated in currencies other than that of the host country or the offshore financial center. [22]

Offshore Financial Centers (OFCs) are jurisdictions where offshore banks are usually exempt from a wide range of regulations which are normally imposed on onshore institutions specifically, deposits are not subject to reserve requirements, bank transactions are mostly tax exempt or treated under a favorable fiscal regime, and they are free of interest and exchange rate restriction, Offshore Banks are generally exempt from regulatory scrutiny with respect

---

[21] Luca Errico and Albert Musalem; *"Offshore Banking: An analysis of Micro-and-Macro-Prudential Issues"*, IMF working Paper WP/99/5, January 1999.

[22] id

to liquidity or capital adequacy, low information disclosure obligations, banking secrecy and anonymity.

The definition of OFC is varied but a jurisdiction will be considered an OFC if it fits any of the following characterizations: [23]

1. Jurisdiction that has relatively large number of financial institutions engaged primary in business with non-residents. [24]
2. Financial System with external assets and liabilities out of proportion to domestic financial intermediation designed to finance domestic economies, [25] and
3. More popularly, centers which provide some or all of the following services; low or zero taxation; moderate or high financial regulation, banking secrecy and anonymity. [26]

It is the third reference, *supra*, that typically offshore Banking is said to take place in 'TAX HAVENS'. Generally a 'tax haven' is a place where certain taxes are levied at a low rate or not al all. There is no official definition of a "tax haven" (sometimes called an "offshore financial center" or OFC), but this term generally is used to describe low-tax economies that attract considerable foreign investment. The United Nations, for instance, defines an offshore institution as "any bank anywhere in the world that accepts deposits and/or manages

---

[23] Monetary and Exchange Affairs Department, IMF Background Paper
[24] id
[25] id
[26] id

assets denominated in foreign currency on behalf of persons legally domiciled elsewhere."[27] The Financial Stability Forum, by contrast, defines OFCs as "jurisdictions that attract a high level of non-resident activity." [28]

The U.S Government Accountability Office December 2008 report on the use of tax havens by American corporations proffered the following characteristics as indicative of a tax haven:[29]

1. No or Nominal taxes.[30]
2. Lack of effective exchange of tax information with foreign tax authorities.[31]
3. Lack of transparency in the operation of legislative, legal or administrative provisions.[32]
4. No requirement for a substantive local presence;[33] and
5. Self—Promotion as an offshore financial center.[34]

The fifth characterizations is worth noting, to the extent that 'Tax Haven's and 'Offshore Financial Centers' are complimentary and interchangeable. Individuals and business entities find it attractive to move themselves or shift assets

---

[27] United Nations, "Financial Havens, Banking Secrecy, and Money Laundering," 1998, at *http://www.imolin.org/finahaeng.htm*

[28] Financial Stability Forum, "Report of the Working Group on Offshore Centers," April 5, 2000. *http://www.fsforum.org*

[29] *Tax Haven,* at *http://www.wikipedia.org*

[30] id

[31] id

[32] id

[33] id

[34] id

to areas with lower tax rates. This creates a situation of Tax competition among governments. Different jurisdictions tend to be havens for different types of taxes, and for different categories of people and business entities.

Tax havens exist all over the world. According to the United Nations Offshore Forum, between 60 and 90 nations and territories participate in the offshore market. [35]The U.S. Department of State lists 52 regimes, including the United States. [36] The OECD, sponsor of a heavily criticized "harmful tax competition" initiative, has identified 41 jurisdictions. [37] The largest OFC, by some measures, is London;[38] others classify America as the world's biggest tax haven. [39]

---

[35] Michael Sesit, *"U.N. Targets Offshore Centers; Plan Aims for minimums standards,"* The Wall Street Journal, January 25, 2000

[36] U.S Department of State, "1999 International Narcotics Control Strategy Report," Bureau for International Narcotics and law Enforcement Affairs, March 2000 at *http://www.state.gov/global/narcotics*

[37] OECD Website, at *http://www.oecd.org*

[38] Financial Stability Forum, "Report of the Working Group on Offshore Centers" at *www.fsforum.org*

[39] Marshall Langer, *"Who Are the Real Tax Haven,"* Tax Notes International, December 18, 2000

HISTORY

There are varied historical accounts as to the origins of Tax Havens of which some are ancient, dating back to 756 when Vatican City had a tax free status. Most economic commentators however suggest that the first "true" tax haven in modern times is Switzerland followed by Liechtenstein. [40]

Swiss banks have long been capital haven for people fleeing social upheaval in Russia, Germany, South America and elsewhere as a result of World War I.[41] It is said that after World War 1, many European countries raised taxes sharply to help pay for reconstruction efforts following the devastation of World War I. Switzerland, having remained neutral during the war, saved itself from reconstruction costs, therefore was able to maintain a low level of taxes. This situation coupled with secrecy laws created by the Swiss government attracted considerable influx of capital from countries affected by the Great World War I.[42]

The OFCs and the Eurocurrency market share a common history, in as much as OFCs are merely the geographical

---

[40] Tax Haven at *www.wikipedia.org*

[41] id

[42] id

extension of the Eurocurrency market outside Western Europe.

OFCs and Eurocurrency centers are essentially the efficient response of international banks to the attempt by sovereign governments in many advanced countries in the 1960s and the 1970s to control capital flows through the imposition of restrictive domestic regulations. These restrictions, which in many cases were intended to provide governments with more control over monetary policy, encouraged a shift of deposits and borrowing to less regulated institutions, essentially banks in OFCs and Euro banks, which are exempt from such restrictions.[43]

In explaining the creation and growth of present-day offshore centers, practitioners and academics put forward at least four factors:[44]

- The establishment of capital controls with a view to reducing unsustainable balance of payments deficits recorded primarily by the United States in the late 1950s and also, by many OECD countries in the 1960s;[45]
- The imposition of high taxes, coupled with a tightening of monetary policy, in an attempt to curb balance of payment deficits resulting from fiscal imbalances, particularly in some OECD countries;[46]

---

[43] Ahmed Zorme, *"Concepts of Offshore Financial Centers: In search of an operational definition."* IMF Working paper WP/07/87, April 2007 at *www.imf.org*

[44] id

[45] id

[46] id

- The removal in 1958 of foreign exchange restrictions on the conversion by nonresidents of current earnings in Western Europe (Johnston, 1982);[47] and
- The fact that U.S. banks' interest in conducting business transactions in foreign currencies and to extend their reach to new territories was spurred by Glass-Steagall Act of 1933, which barred commercial banks from entering the investment banking business.[48]

Thus, the combined effect of increasingly restrictive regulatory regimes onshore and new business opportunities abroad engendered by the return to full convertibility of nonresident assets in Europe provided an impetus to financial institutions and large multinational corporations to delocalize and increase the volume of their financial activities offshore. It is this massive delocalization that contributed to broaden and deepen the scope of markets in international currencies that are now known as the Eurocurrency market.[49] For the United States, for instance, these measures included the Interest Equalization Tax (1963), the Voluntary Foreign Credit Restraint (1965), and the Foreign Direct Investment Program (1965), all aimed at limiting the ability of U.S. banks to lend to foreigners.[50] Tight monetary policy was achieved by imposing domestic capital restrictions, such as reserve requirements and interest rate ceilings (with the intention

---

[47] id

[48] Ahmed Zorme, "*Concepts of Offshore Financial Centers: In search of an operational definition.*" IMF Working paper WP/07/87, April 2007 at *www.imf.org*

[49] id

[50] id

of limiting banks' credit through their capacity to mobilize deposits).[51]

Throughout the 1960s and the 1970s, the Eurocurrency market grew at a remarkable pace.[52] The shift of financial activities to Eurocurrencies gained considerable momentum after 1966, when U.S. money market rates rose above the interest rate ceilings on dollar deposits allowed by Regulation Q, resulting in a credit crunch that, in turn, forced U.S. banks to seek funds in the Eurodollar market (Cassard, 1994). During 1966-77, the gross size of the Euromarket—that is, the sum of all Eurocurrency liabilities, including interbank deposits—grew 17-fold, from US$18 billion at end-1966 to US$310 billion at end-1977 (Dufey and Giddy, 1978).[53]

In the early 1970s, the geographical location of the market shifted from being mainly Western European to worldwide. Banks and, later, securities and insurance firms began setting up offshore branches in a number of jurisdictions in the Caribbean, Latin America and Southeast Asia. It is these jurisdictions that have become known today as offshore financial centers. [54]

---

[51] id

[52] id

[53] Ahmed Zorme, *"Concepts of Offshore Financial Centers: In search of an operational definition."* IMF Working paper WP/07/87, April 2007 at *www.imf.org*

[54] id

SIGNIFICANCE OF OFC ACTIVITIES IN THE INTERNATIONAL FINANCIAL SYSTEM

While incomplete (there are no worldwide statistics for securities and IBCs) and with the limitations inherent to OFC data collection, the available statistics nevertheless indicate that offshore banking business remain sizeable. [55]

Calculations based on BIS data suggest that, by end-December 2003, the external position of offshore banks in terms of assets (in accordance with the BIS list) had reached US$1.9 trillion, compared with US$16 trillion of total bank assets. [56] By the same date, external loans (i.e., claims of OFCs on the rest of the world) had reached US$1.5 trillion or 13 percent of the world cross-border bank claims, as reported to the BIS (US$11.9 trillion). However, because not all banks or OFCs report to the BIS, it is more likely that these figures are underestimated. [57]

---

[55] Ahmed Zorme, "*Concepts of Offshore Financial Centers: In search of an operational definition.*" IMF Working paper WP/07/87, April 2007 at *www.imf.org*

[56] id

[57] id

Regarding securities, although OFCs are recognized as significant hubs for the administration of mutual funds, assets under management in OFCs are estimated at around US$400 billion, a rather small portion of the assets managed worldwide (estimated at US$12 trillion) (Dixon, 2001).[58]

In the insurance sector, publicly available worldwide consolidated data are scarce.[59] Bermuda, the leading OFC and the world's largest captive insurance center, reported in 2001 some 1,600 insurance and reinsurance companies totaling $172 billion in assets, and underwriting over $48 billion in annual gross premiums (IMF, 2005).[60] Furthermore, for the first time, in 2004, Bermuda became the fourth-largest reinsurance market in the world, after the United Sates, Germany, and Switzerland (in terms of total net written premiums). Under Regulation Q, ceilings were imposed on the level of interest rates banks were permitted to pay on deposit in the United States (but not their branches abroad).[61] Based on BIS data, on-balance-sheet OFC cross-border assets reached US$4.6 trillion at end-June 1999 (about 50 percent of total cross-border assets), of which US$0.9 trillion in the Caribbean. (IMF, 2000).[62]

---

[58] id

[59] id

[60] Ahmed Zorme, *"Concepts of Offshore Financial Centers: In search of an operational definition."* IMF Working paper WP/07/87, April 2007 at *www.imf.org*

[61] Ahmed Zorme, *"Concepts of Offshore Financial Centers: In search of an operational definition."* IMF Working paper WP/07/87, April 2007 at *www.imf.org*

[62] id

HOW IS OFFSHORE
FINANCE CARRIED OUT?

Banking activity in OFCs is now predominantly carried out by branches and affiliates of banks incorporated elsewhere, mainly in major countries, but also in larger emerging market economies.[63] Since the failure of BCCI and Meridian Bank it has become difficult for a bank incorporated in a jurisdiction with limited domestic markets to carry on business in other countries.[64] Supervisors now require banks wishing to open branches and affiliates to demonstrate a capacity for their home supervisor to exert consolidated supervision, which it is almost impossible to do for a bank whose business is almost entirely outside the home country's jurisdiction.[65]

The physical presence of establishments of foreign banks in OFCs varies.[66] In some centers they may originate and, in some cases, fund the business carried on their books.[67] But in

---

[63] Monetary and Exchange Affairs Department, IMF Background Paper
[64] id
[65] id
[66] id
[67] id

other cases, they may have a very limited physical presence and the business decisions may all be taken elsewhere.[68] Such establishments are sometimes known as *"shell" branches*.[69] There has been a tendency in the more successful OFCs for the amount of local value added to grow, as these OFCs have acquired the ability to supply specialist capabilities and skills.[70] Offshore activities may also take place through so-called *parallel-owned banks,* that is, banks that are not subsidiaries of a bank in the onshore center, but have the same owners or controllers. Effective consolidated supervision is more difficult in such cases.[71]

Offshore banks engage in a wide variety of transactions: foreign currency loans (including syndicated loans) and the taking of deposits, the issue of securities, over-the counter (OTC) trading in derivatives for risk-management and speculative purposes, and the management of customers' financial assets.[72]

- Foreign currency lending and its associated funding. This is normally an asset driven business, sometimes originated in the OFC, but often originated elsewhere and booked and funded in the OFC, normally for tax reasons. Sometimes the funding is arranged by the office originating the loan, but sometimes it may be

---

[68] id

[69] id

[70] Monetary and Exchange Affairs Department, IMF Background Paper

[71] Monetary and Exchange Affairs Department, IMF Background Paper

[72] id

---

arranged by the entity in the OFC itself. This funding activity gives rise to a substantial volume of inter-bank activity, sometimes, but not always, between branches and affiliates of the same bank. At end-June 1999, about 70 percent of OFC banks' cross-border assets and about 60 percent of cross-border liabilities were vis-à-vis other banks. The risks involved in this activity are normally managed by the banks' main offices. [73]

- A significant proportion of Eurobonds floated in international capital markets is also issued in OFCs, although the marketing and selling of such instruments would normally be done in major financial markets. Recently, the use of special purpose vehicles registered in OFCs has led to a growing volume of structured finance deals, which again mainly for tax reasons are domiciled in OFCs. Over the period 1992-98, the outstanding amount of international money market instruments (bonds and notes) issued in OFCs grew at an average annual rate of 23 percent, somewhat faster than such issuance in the world as a whole. At end-June 1999, they stood at some US$1 trillion or 21 percent of total international money market instruments.[74]

- The use of OTC derivative instruments blossomed over the last decade, but was mainly concentrated in a few primary IFCs. Because derivatives entail substantive counterparty, settlement, liquidity and legal risks they require the infrastructure of developed financial centers, where their use is more prevalent. Among IFCs, the use

---

[73] id

[74] Monetary and Exchange Affairs Department, IMF Background Paper

of over-the-counter trading in derivatives is thought to have increased in the U.S. IBFs, the JOM, and to a certain extent in OFCs with major financial markets. But in other cases derivative transactions arranged elsewhere may be booked in an OFC if tax or other reasons make that more profitable.[75]

- Deposit taking from individual customers is an activity specialized in by a number of OFCs. Normally, the banks involved in this business are major international banks with a high reputation (deposit insurance is normally not available).[76] The attraction is normally related to tax, both income and capital taxes. The proceeds of this type of business are normally invested in high quality marketable assets in major financial centers.[77] While some of this business is on-balance sheet, the part that is probably growing fastest is in funds managed by financial institutions and marketed in major centers.[78] In addition, as noted above, OFCs are used for the management of personal funds in a variety of trusts and other forms, some managed by financial institutions but some managed by law firms and other specialists.[79]

---

[75] id

[76] id

[77] id

[78] Monetary and Exchange Affairs Department, IMF Background Paper

[79] id

REASONS FOR OFFSHORE BANKING

Offshore Banking has been an increasingly attractive alternative to the sometimes heavily regulated financial markets.[80] Offshore banks seem to exploit the risk—return trade off by being more profitable than onshore banks, and in many instances also more leveraged.[81]

The following are a number of legitimate factors that tend to attract Financial Institution and investors to OFC's.[82]

1. More convenient fiscal regimes with lower explicit taxation and increase net profit margins.[83]
2. Convenient regulatory frameworks that reduce implicit taxation also increasing profit margins.[84]

---

[80] Financial Stability Forum, "Report of the Working Group on Offshore Centers," April 5, 2000. *http://www.fsforum.org*

[81] id

[82] id

[83] id

[84] id

3. Minimum formalities for incorporation.[85]
4. Adequate legal framework that safeguards the integrity of principal agent relation.[86]
5. Proximity to major financial centers.[87]
6. The reputation of the particular OFC.[88]
7. Complete freedom from exchange controls.[89]

Countries may decide to establish OFCs for the following number of reasons:[90]

1. Access to International Capital Markets.[91]
2. Attracting needed foreign technical expertise and skills.[92]
3. Introducing an element of competition in domestic financial systems, while at the some time, somewhat sheltering domestic institutions.[93]
4. To benefit from related income-generating activities and the creation of new jobs.[94]

---

[85] id
[86] id
[87] id
[88] id
[89] Monetary and Exchange Affairs Department, IMF Background Paper
[90] Financial Stability Forum, "Report of the Working Group on Offshore Centers," April 5, 2000. *http://www.fsforum.org*
[91] id
[92] id
[93] id
[94] id

Most OFC's are countries but some important OFC's are located within the border of countries, such as the U.S International Banking Facilities, the Japanese offshore market, the Bangkok International Banking Facilities in Thailand, and Lubuan International Offshore Center in Malaysia.[95]

---

[95] Monetary and Exchange Affairs Department, IMF Background Paper

ADVANTAGES (USES) OF OFFSHORE FINANCIAL CENTERS

Offshore Banking Licenses: A multinational corporation sets up an offshore bank to handle its foreign exchange operations or to facilitate financing of an international joint venture.[96] An onshore bank establishes a wholly owned subsidiary in an OFC to provide offshore fund administration services (e.g. fully integrated global custody, fund accounting, fund administration, and transfer agent services).[97] The owner of a regulated onshore bank establishes a sister, "Parallel" bank in an OFC.[98] The attractions of the OFC may include no capital tax, no withholding tax on dividends or interest, no tax on transfers, no corporation tax, no capital gains tax, no exchange controls, light supervision, less stringent reporting requirement, and stringent trading restrictions.[99]

Offshore Corporations or International Business Corporations (IBCs): IBCs are limited liability vehicles

---

[96] Financial Stability Forum, "Report of the Working Group on Offshore Centers," April 5, 2000. *http://www.fsforum.org*

[97] id

[98] id

[99] id

registered in an OFC. They may be used to own and operate businesses, issue shares or bonds, or raise capital in other ways.[100] IBCs may be set up with one director only.[101] In some cases, residents of the OFC host country may act as nominee directors to conceal the identity of the true company directors. In some OFCs, bearer share certificates may be used.[102] In other OFCs, registered shares certificates are used, but no public registry of shareholders in maintained.[103] In many OFCs, the costs of setting up IBCs are minimal and they are generally exempt from all taxes. IBCs are popular vehicle for managing investment funds.[104]

Insurance Companies: A commercial corporation establishes a captive insurance company in an OFC to manage risk and minimize taxes.[105] An onshore insurance company establishes a subsidiary in an OFC to reinsure certain risks underwritten by the parent and reduce overall reserve and capital requirements.[106] An onshore reinsurance company incorporates a subsidiary in an OFC to reinsure catastrophic risks. The attractions of an OFC in these circumstances include favorable income withholding/capital tax regime and low or weakly enforced actuarial reserve requirements and capital standards.[107]

Special Purpose Vehicle: One of the most rapidly growing uses of OFCs is the use of Special Purpose Vehicles (SPVs)

---

[100] id

[101] id

[102] id

[103] Financial Stability Forum, "Report of the Working Group on Offshore Centers," April 5, 2000. *http://www.fsforum.org*

[104] id

[105] id

[106] id

[107] id

to engage in financial activities in a more favorable tax environment.[108] An onshore corporation establishes an IBC in an OFC to engage in a specific activity.[109] The issuance of asset—backed securities is the most frequently cited activity of SPVs.[110] The onshore corporation may assign a set of assets to the offshore SPV (e.g., a portfolio of mortgages, loans, credit card receivables).[111] The SPV then offers a variety of securities to investors based on the underlying assets. The SPV, and hence the onshore parent, benefit from the favorable tax treatment in the OFC. Financial institutions also make use of SPVs to take advantage of less restrictive regulations on their activities.[112] Banks, in particular, use them to raise Tier I capital in the lower tax environments of OFCs.[113] SPVs are also set up by non-bank financial institutions to take advantage of more liberal netting rules than faced in home countries, reducing their capital requirements.[114]

Asset Management and Protection: Wealthy individuals and enterprise in countries with weak economies and fragile banking systems may want to keep assets overseas to protect them against the collapse of their domestic currencies and domestic banks, and outside the reach of existing or potential exchange controls.[115] If these individuals also seek confidentiality, then an account in an OFC is often the

---

[108] id

[109] id

[110] id

[111] id

[112] Financial Stability Forum, "Report of the Working Group on Offshore Centers," April 5, 2000. *http://www.fsforum.org*

[113] id

[114] id

[115] id

vehicle of choice. In some cases, fear of wholesale seizures of legitimately acquired assets is also a motive for going to an OFC.[116] In this case, confidentiality is very important. Also, many individuals facing unlimited liability in their home jurisdictions seek to restructure ownership of their assets through offshore trusts to protect those assets from onshore lawsuits.[117] Some OFCs have legislation in place that protects those who transfer property to a personal trust from forced inheritance provisions in their home countries.[118]

Tax Planning: Wealthy individuals make use of favorable tax environments in, and tax treaties with, OFCs, often involving offshore companies, trusts and foundations.[119] There is also a range of schemes that, while legally defensible, rely on complexity and ambiguity, often involving types of trusts not available in the client's country of residence. Multinational Companies' route activities through low tax OFCs to minimize their total tax bill through transfer pricing, i.e. goods may be made onshore but invoices are issued offshore by an IBC owned by the multinational, moving onshore profits to low tax regimes.[120]

* Offshore banks can sometimes provide access to politically and economically stable jurisdictions.[121] This will be an advantage for residents in areas where there

---

[116] id

[117] id

[118] Financial Stability Forum, "Report of the Working Group on Offshore Centers," April 5, 2000. *http://www.fsforum.org*

[119] id

[120] id

[121] Sovereign Society Offshore A-Letter at *http://www. sovereignsociety.com* / offshore banking

is risk of political turmoil, who fear their assets may be frozen, seized or disappear (Corralito for example, during the 2001 Argentine economic crisis). [122] However, developed countries with regulated banking systems offer the same advantages in terms of stability.[123]

* Some offshore banks may operate with a lower cost base and can provide higher interest rates than the legal rate in the home country due to lower overheads and a lack of government intervention.[124] Advocates of offshore banking often characterize government regulation as a form of tax on domestic banks, reducing interest rates on deposits. [125]

* Offshore finance is one of the few industries, along with tourism, in which geographically remote island nations can competitively engage.[126] It can help developing countries source investment and create growth in their economies, and can help redistribute world finance from the developed to developing world.[127]

* Interest is generally paid by offshore banks without tax being deducted.[128] This is an advantage to individuals who do not pay tax on worldwide income, or who do not pay tax until the tax return is agreed, or who feel

---

[122] id

[123] id

[124] Financial Stability Forum, "Report of the Working Group on Offshore Centers," April 5, 2000. *http://www.fsforum.org*

[125] id

[126] id

[127] id

[128] id

that they can illegally evade tax by hiding the interest income.[129]

* Some offshore banks offer banking services that may not be available from domestic banks such as anonymous bank accounts, higher or lower rate loans based on risk and investment opportunities not available elsewhere.[130]

* Offshore banking is often linked to other structures, such as offshore companies, trusts or foundations, which may have specific tax advantages for some individuals.[131]

* Many advocates of offshore banking also assert that the creation of tax and banking competition is to an advantage of the industry. Tax and Banking competition allows people to choose an appropriate balance of services and taxes.[132]

* Diversify your investment portfolio with foreign currencies and maximize your returns whether the dollar soars or gets crushed.[133]

* Earn the highest yields on earth. No matter where they may be offered.[134]

* Escape the dangers of being tied to the dollar when you diversify into elite investments unknown to ordinary U.S investors.[135]

---

[129] id

[130] id

[131] Financial Stability Forum, "Report of the Working Group on Offshore Centers," April 5, 2000. *http://www.fsforum.org*

[132] id

[133] id

[134] id

[135] id

* Protect your retirement from legal or government actions by taking your IRA offshore with more favorable conditions.[136]

* Expand your portfolio to include international stocks your broker will never tell you about. Companies that far out perform their U.S counterparts.[137]

* Access the out-performing power of global hedge fund and do it for far less than the normally—prohibitive minimums.[138]

* Reach beyond the domestic market when planning real estate investments.[139]

* Secure your wealth behind an impenetrable shield of protection. Never be harassed by ex-business partners, ex-spouses, ex-clients or anyone else who would take what's rightfully yours.[140]

* Keep your wealth with the ones you want—not the government—even after you're gone, by setting up the proper asset protection trust—(*Right and Freedom of contract*).[141]

* Add another layer of security to one's identity by obtaining rapid residency and second passport. This facilitates travel better.[142]

---

[136] id

[137] Financial Stability Forum, "Report of the Working Group on Offshore Centers," April 5, 2000. *http://www.fsforum.org*

[138] Financial Stability Forum, "Report of the Working Group on Offshore Centers," April 5, 2000. *http://www.fsforum.org*

[139] id

[140] id

[141] id

[142] id

DISADVANTAGES (MISUSES) OF OFFSHORE BANKING

Tax Evasion—There are individuals and enterprises that rely on banking secrecy and opaque corporate structures to avoid declaring assets and income to relevant tax authorities. This is a disadvantage to the sovereign but an advantage to the payer.[143]

Money Laundering—Individuals and enterprises moving money gained from illegal transactions or fraudulent market activities seek maximum secrecy to avoid criminal and supervisory investigation.[144]

---

[143] Financial Stability Forum, "Report of the Working Group on Offshore Centers," April 5, 2000. *http://www.fsforum.org*

[144] id

CURRENT ISSUES WITH OFFSHORE BANKING AND TAX HAVENS

In recent times organizations such as the United Nations, Financial Stability Forum (FSF), Financial Action Task Force on Money laundering (FATF), Organization of European Cooperation and Development (OECD), Tax Justice Network (TJN) and the present Obama administration together with G-20 have advocated for the 'closure' of all Tax havens due to its probative effects on tax evasion and money laundering primarily due to 'bank secrecy'.

Bank secrecy is in recent times an area of dispute between two groups of countries: one group that permits its banks to keep depositors' identities secret, and the rest of the world that wants to enforce taxation of the income earned by those accounts. The U.S. is part of the group that is demanding more information about account holders so that it can tax the income of Americans who keep their money overseas. And in fact, while some U.S. individuals with foreign bank accounts dutifully report their foreign income, some take advantage of the host country's bank secrecy laws to hide taxable income. This appears to be the issue predicating the recent legal tussle between the United States government and Union Bank of Switzerland (UBS).While bank secrecy is principally about individuals who fail to report taxable income; the issue is often raised in discussions of international tax reform although there is only a limited connection. Bank secrecy is just one of many government policies that may contribute to a nation being labeled a "tax haven." The prominent issue is whether any nation's policies undermine another's tax enforcement.

Cooperative agreements among nations, such as the OECD's Harmful Tax Practice initiative launched in 1996, have addressed such concerns by urging more information disclosure to ease tax enforcement. The OECD Harmful Tax Practice initiative criticizes four aspects of countries' tax systems:[145]

- The use of preferential tax regimes that include a zero rate or very low tax rate. [146]
- A lack of transparency.[147]
- The absence of information exchange with other countries (of particular import to the bank secrecy issue),[148] and
- "ring-fencing," i.e., giving tax benefits to foreign investors that are denied to domestic residents.[149]

Of the 47 regimes initially identified as problematic, most have subsequently been changed to satisfy the OECD. Of the 33 non-OECD countries and jurisdictions cited as providing

---

[145] Jeffrey Owens, *"OECD's work in counteracting the use of Tax Havens to evade Taxes,"* OECD, Center for Tax Policy and Administration, December 11, 2006, pg 3.

[146] id

[147] id

[148] id

[149] id

---

inadequate information, only five remained on the list after 2004.[150]

The United Nations Office for Drug Control and Crime Prevention for instance, remarked that "Offshore financial Centers can be used for dubious purposes such as tax evasion and money laundering, by taking advantage of a higher potential for less transparent operating environments, including a higher level of anonymity, to escape the notice of the law enforcement agencies in the home country of the beneficial owner of the funds".[151]

The April 2000 FSF report on offshore centers highlighted prudential and market integrity concerns stemming from factors in OFCs that impede effective supervision by the onshore home supervisor and hinder cooperation, which is necessary to enhance financial stability and fight financial fraud.[152]

In 2000, the FATF undertook an initiative to identify non-cooperative countries and territories in the fight against money laundering. The FATF's first review (June 2000) named 15 jurisdictions, including 12 OFCs, as having critical deficiencies in their anti-money laundering systems. Since that review, all but three offshore centers have made significant and rapid progress in addressing deficiencies and have been

---

[150] "Which Countries Become Tax Havens?" NBER, working paper No. 12802, December 2006, pg 7.

[151] Financial Havens, Banking Secrecy and Money Laundering, U.N Office for Drug Control and Crime Prevention, Global Program Against Money Laundering(U.N., 1998)

[152] Salim M. Darbs, R. Barry Johnston, and Mary G. Zephrin, "Filling a gap in global surveillance", Finance and Development September 2003, p.34.

---

removed from the list. The OECD has pursued a project on harmful tax practices that affect OFCs, among others. In 2002, the OECD made public a list of 7 uncooperative tax havens that included 6 OFCs; about 30 other OFCs had made commitments to transparency and effective exchange of information.[153]

The IMF has significantly stepped up its surveillance of financial systems in recent years to identify potential financial vulnerabilities, including those resulting from weakness in supervisory and regulatory systems. Traditionally, economic policies of its member countries are monitored by the IMF as part of its surveillance process, and while some OFCs are members, many are nonmembers or dependent territories of members and are thus excluded from IMF surveillance. The IMF's role in OFCs was considered by its Executive Board in 2000 in context of the IMF's mandate to promote financial stability. At that time, the Board noted that there was limited evidence on the direct risks to the global financial system posed by OFCs. They also noted, however, that when standards for supervision are inadequate and comprehensive risk analysis is hampered by a lack of reliable data on activities in OFCs, there can be risks to financial stability. In response, the IMF designed the OFC program, which has two broad components: financial supervision, comprising assessments and technical assistance and statistics.[154]

The U.S. IRS has estimated that it looses $70 billion a year in revenue because of investments and monies placed in

---

[153] id

[154] Salim M. Darbs, R. Barry Johnston, and Mary G. Zephrin, "Filling a gap in global surveillance", Finance and Development September 2003, p.34.

offshore financial centers when combined with the revenue lost from other nations, it is understandable that there is a concerted effort to access confidential financial information in order to recover revenue.[155]

Following the horrific events of September 11, 2001, the United States and its international allies have escalated their resolve to crackdown on offshore confidentiality. Though loosely associated with money laundering prior to September 11th attacks, terrorist financing has become the focus of many money laundering statutes and investigations. Ironically though, there is evidence that the September 11th terrorist laundered most of their monies through onshore financial centers, such as London.[156]

Nonetheless, the United States and the International Community have passed resolutions as well as statutes, and have conducted themselves in a manner that is destined to shatter offshore confidentiality protections. Examples of such are USA Patriot Act, US IRS Qualified Intermediary (QI) requirements, Mutual Legal Assistance Treaties (MLATS), and the European Union Withholding Tax (July, 2005).

On June 23, 2006 the New York Times, the Wall Street Journal and the Los Angeles Times all revealed that there was a terrorist tracking program by the US Treasury and CIA to access SWIFT transaction database, which in effect broaches bank secrecies that offshore banks are noted for.

---

[155] G. Scott Dowling, Fatal Broadside: *"The Demise of Caribbean Offshore Financial Confidentiality Post USA Patriot Act"* 17 Transnational lawyer, 2004

[156] id

Senator Charles Schummer used the U.S terrorist attacks as an opportunity to attack low tax jurisdiction by arguing that "financial privacy laws conceal illegal activity".[157]

The German external intelligence services recent purchase of confidential client data stolen from a Liechtenstein bank and recent legal tussle between the United States government and Union Bank of Switzerland (UBS), further attests OECD members resolve in demanding than tax havens loosen their Privacy Laws so that foreign tax collectors can track and tax funds invested in lower-tax jurisdictions.

---

[157] Senator Charles Shummer, "Websites Enable Terrorist cells to launder money in off-shore banks, Obtain Fake Passports," press release, September 26, 2001, at *http://www.senate.gov*

ANALYSIS

From the foregoing, it is very obvious that the advantage of Offshore Banking far outweighs the disadvantages. Offshore Banks are providing services consistent with the seven functions of the Global financial system.

Business conducted in OFCs covers a wide range of financial sectors, such as banking, insurance and securities.

Banking is the most prevalent business in the OFCs. Most banks located in OFCs are branches or subsidiaries of international banks. Their main activity is collecting deposits from various markets and channeling them back to their parent institutions. Private banking is a major service offered to high-net-worth persons. Specialized services for such clients include asset management, estate planning, foreign exchange trading and Pension arrangement. Some banks also provide non-bank services, such as custodian and trustee services.

Collective investment schemes (mutual funds and hedge funds) are also domiciled in OFCs, mainly for tax purposes. Related fund activities such as allocation of assets, fund distribution, asset management, fund administration, custodian services, and back-office work are also conducted in these centers.

A large number of Special Purpose Vehicles (SPVs), which are increasingly used by financial and non-financial corporations, are registered in the OFCs. Financial firms use SPV for securitization, and non-financial corporations use them to lower the cost of raising capital. OFCs are attractive places to register SPVs because of the tax advantages they offer, which are supported by a facilitating regulatory regime.

Insurance business including life, reinsurance (insurance companies that assume all or part of a risk undertaken by other insurance companies), and captive (companies owned by non-insurance firms that provide insurance coverage to the owners) is also conducted in some OFCs. Innovative regulatory and legal environments have helped offshore centers attract a large share of the world's reinsurance market. A large portion of the world's captive insurance companies (which may do reinsurance) is also domiciled in these centers.

Asset protection, including trusts, is another service offered by OFCs. Reasons for managing assets in OFCs include protection from weak domestic banks or currencies, additional legal protection from lawsuits in the home jurisdictions, and tax avoidance.

The activities described above and others are often undertaken through international business companies (IBCs, or exempt companies) and trust arrangements. In many offshore centers, the costs of setting up IBCs are minimal, and their activities are generally exempt from taxes.

This issue however is whether the two major concerns (*money laundering and tax evasion/unfair tax competition*) of the United States, OECD, the United Nations and others are enough to discredit and disallow offshore banking, meaning shutting down Tax havens.

The extent of illegal activity in offshore banking is greatly overstated and sensationalized. While some illegal activities do occur offshore, the vast majority of investors are legitimate. In addition many offshore centers are well regulated, have enacted measures to reduce criminal activity and view misuse of confidentiality as a threat to their economic stability. It is argued that the Bahamian money laundering statute may be more modern than those of most nations, including the United States.[158]

Ironically many onshore banking systems have been victims of elaborate money laundering schemes.

On May 30, 2008, the Executive Board of the International Monetary Fund agreed to integrate the offshore financial center (OFC) assessment program with the Financial Sector Assessment Program (FSAP). The Directors agreed that OFC's compliance with standards is generally comparable with that of non-OFC organizations.[159]

The claim that financial Privacy Laws of offshore centers conceal illegal activities is unfortunately, a false stereotype. To the contrary, Low-tax nations are not filled with criminals carrying cash filled suitcases. Tax havens do attract wealth, of course, but most of the money is institutional investment. Bermuda, for instance, is the world's largest center for captive insurance companies. Luxembourg leads the world in managing the most mutual fund assets. The Cayman Islands meanwhile, is second in both of those categories. American corporations also make extensive use of offshore regimes, earning almost one-third of their profits in low-tax jurisdictions.[160]

Individual investors also utilize tax havens, but little of this capital has criminal origins. Instead, it represents legitimate investment by people seeking sound money management, asset protection, and lower tax bills. This last feature is controversial, but only because many high-tax nations assert

---

[158] Tax Haven at *www.wikipedia.org*
[159] IMF, Public Information Notice (PIN) No. 08/82, July 9, 2008
[160] "Gimme Shelter," The Economist, January 29, 2000

the right to tax income earned outside their borders and get upset because low-tax jurisdictions usually refuse to act as vassal tax collectors.

This is not to say that there is no money laundering in tax havens, but it does suggest that those who do it are minor players. After all, criminals rarely venture "offshore" because of the added risk. Shifting money across borders-and then back again when the funds are needed-dramatically increases the probability of detection. The United Nations has acknowledged that criminals avoid so-called tax havens because they are a "red flag" for law enforcement.[161] I agree with this UN acknowledgment because one of the 'red flags' for the U.S Customs and Immigration (ICE) is where one has visited before entering the United States. One is likely to be further examined depending on where one has visited and whether that destination is on the government's 'watch list'.

Ironically, the OECD inadvertently confirms that there is no link between tax havens and money laundering. As part of its "harmful tax competition" initiative, the OECD identified so-called tax havens, which it has threatened with financial protectionism if they do not join its proposed cartel. Yet less than one-fifth of these OECD-identified low-tax jurisdictions and none of the major offshore financial centers are on the list of 19 "non-cooperative" money laundering jurisdictions put together by the OECD's own Financial Action Task Force.[162]

---

[161] Financial Havens, Banking Secrecy and Money Laundering, U.N Office for Drug Control and Crime Prevention, Global Program Against Money Laundering(U.N., 1998)

[162] Financial Action Task Force, "List of Non-Cooperative Countries and Territories," at *http://www1.oecd.org/fatf/ NCCT_en.htm*

According to the OECD's Financial Action Task Force, "criminal funds" are usually processed relatively close to the under-lying activity; often in the country where the funds originate.[163] This situation suggests that money laundering occurs in America and Europe for the simple reason that these are the regions where criminals obtain most of their loot. Indeed, according to an article in Government Executive, "The International Monetary Fund estimates that about $600 billion is laundered each year globally. Estimates of U.S money-laundering traffic hover at $300 billion, including about $60 billion in drug money alone".[164]

The plethora of laws designed to fight dirty money seems to have little effect. The Treasury Department has estimated that 99.9 percent of criminal money in the United States is laundered successfully.[165] Other countries such as Germany have reached similar conclusions about their own financial systems.

Part of the problem is that law enforcement resources are not well-targeted. Money laundering laws already require millions of reports on the financial practices of law-abiding citizens, forcing law enforcement to search for a needle in a haystack. Proposals to expand these laws will make haystack even bigger. A recent article in the London Times outlines this

---

[163] Financial Action Task Force, "Basic Facts About Money Laundering." www1.oecd.org.org/fatf/mlaundering_en.htm

[164] Julie Wakefield, *"Following the money,"* Government Executive, October 1, 2000.

[165] Raymond Baker, *"Money Laundering and Flight Capital: The Impact on Private Banking,"* testimony before the permanent subcommittee on Investigations, committee on Governmental Affairs, U.S Senate, November 10 1999.

quandary: "Sifting through millions of financial transactions or placing onerous burdens on banks, accountants and lawyers to report "suspicious" activity is of questionable efficacy in the fight against money-laundering. It makes the obligation of public authorities passive: in this model they await reports from bank managers, accountants, lawyers and other professionals, rather than taking active steps to deploy crime-fighters to identify, pursue and indict criminals".[166]

In the United States, financial institutions filed about 13 million currency transaction reports in 1999 at a cost to the industry of more than $100 million.[167] This "ever-increasing regulatory burden on the banking industry" would be acceptable if it led to less crime, but that does not seem to be the result. According to government figures, less than 1/1000th of the 1 percent of currency reports is ever used in money-laundering conviction. [168]

A recent Washington Post story uses the September 11 attacks to explain the problems law enforcement faces: "The FBI has told Congress that terrorists rely heavily on wire transfers, but detecting suspicious transfers can be nearly impossible, banking sources say. A large bank might typically

---

[166] Graham Mather, *"Money-Laundering Flight Could Hit the Wrong Targets,"* The Times(UK), October 2, 2001 at *http://www.thetimes.co.uk*

[167] Ron Paul, Tom Campell, Bob Barr, and Walter Jones, "Report Together with Dissenting Views[to accompany H.R. 3886]" Committee on Banking, U.S. House of Representatives, 106th Congress, 2nd sess., July 11, 2000

[168] Edward Yingling, "ABA Statement on House Banking Committee Approval on Money Laundering Act," American Bankers Association, June 8, 2000

handle 10,000 to 125,000 wire transfers per day. About 70 percent are for amounts less than $500,000, though sums of $1 million to $4 million are not unusual. So even the opening money transfer of $100,000 to [terrorist Mohammed] Atta would not have seemed unusual, officials said. Investigators do not believe any bank made a major error in failing to follow guidelines for detecting or reporting suspicious activities. "Nothing they did would have tipped anyone off," said one source".[169]

---

[169] Ron Paul, Tom Campell, Bob Barr, and Walter Jones, "Report Together with Dissenting Views[to accompany H.R. 3886]" Committee on Banking, U.S. House of Representatives, 106th Congress, 2nd sess., July 11, 2000

CONCLUSION

Offshore Banking is of immense value to the global financial system. It facilitates multi-national entities as well as other investors to develop their efficiencies by moving into low tax jurisdictions where they can also enjoy financial privacy. Multi-National and individuals have a right to mitigate their tax burdens. In Gregory V. Helvering, 29 U.S. 465, the U.S. Supreme Court Stated that "The legal right of an individual to decrease the amount of what would otherwise be his taxes or altogether avoid them by means which the law permits, cannot be doubted".

The importance of banking confidentially can be traced back to before Roman times, when temples acted as banks making financial confidentiality vital to an individual's privacy. Banking transactions reflects a person's lifestyle, personal interest and political beliefs. Historically, the common law imposed a duty of confidentiality on banks regarding financial records. In Tournier v. National Provincial Bank, [1924] 1 K. B. 461, C.A., the court in England held that bankers had a contracted duty not to disclose a client's financial information. We have the right to privacy, self preservation and freedom to contract and flee from despots. Secret accounts were useful to anyone being persecuted by Nazis, citizens of communist regimes, and anyone else who didn't trust their government not to confiscate their wealth.

There is nothing criminal with a jurisdiction taxing zero or low tax. In fact John Arthur Laffer, a notable economist postulates that "tax cuts create an incentive to increase output, employment and production, they also help balance the budget by reducing means-tested government expenditures. A faster growing economy means lower unemployment and higher incomes, resulting in reduced unemployment benefits and other social welfare programs".[170]

A recent study finds that from 1982 to 1999 countries with low tax rates grew 2.5 times faster—3.3 percent annually compared to 1.4 percent for the world economy.[171] In 1994 Estonia for example became the first European country to adopt a flat tax and its 26 percent flat tax dramatically energized what had been faltering economy. Before adopting the flat tax, Estonian economy was literally shrinking. In the eight years after 1994, Estonia experienced real economic growth—averaging 5.2 percent per year. Latvia, Lithuania, and Russia have also adopted flat taxes with similar success-sustained economic growth and increasing tax revenues.[172]

International companies operate on integrated, global basis to be as competitive as possible. Neutral tax policy allows companies to pursue their competitiveness strategies without artificial incentives or disincentives from tax policy. Consequently, the companies become stronger, more flexible and better able to expand at home and abroad. This is also

---

[170] Dan Egger and Kathleen Day, "The U.S. Ties Hijackers' Money to Al Qaeda," The Washington Port, October 7, 2001, *www. washingtonpost.com*

[171] Laffer Curve at *www.wikipedia.org*

[172] James R. Huns, *"Do Tax Havens Flourish?"* Tax Policy and the Economy, Vol. 19 (Cambridge, MA:MIT Press, 2005) p. 66

consistent with 'Business Judgment Rules' that courts don't disturb. Moreover, Tax Havens, so called have right to self determination. It is out of place for Tax Havens to give up 'bank secrecy' protections to enforce another jurisdiction's tax laws, however, 'Mutual Legal Assistance Treaties' based upon international Law Principle of 'Dual Criminality' is acceptable, based upon public interest, which is also an exclusion under *Tournier, supra*.

The links between money laundering activities and offshore financial centers have not been established at least per IMF estimates (*indicated supra*). It rather appears most of the money laundering takes place onshore rather.

According to Daniel J. Mitchell, a senior fellow specializing in tax issues and author of "The Flat Tax freedom, Fairness, Jobs and Growth", we are all beneficiaries of tax havens in ways you might not expect. [173] "First, if you live in a developed country, your taxes are probably much lower today than they were 30 years ago, thanks in part to tax havens. In 1980, top personal income tax rates in OECD countries averaged more than 67 percent, and corporate rates that year averaged nearly 50 percent. To compound the damage, countries routinely imposed extra layers of tax on capital, including dividend taxes, capital gains taxes, inheritance taxes, and wealth taxes. These policies discouraged saving and investment, stifling economic growth and causing significant economic hardship.

Beginning with Reagan and Thatcher, however, governments have been racing to cut tax rates and reform tax regimes. Top personal tax rates now average only about 40 percent, and corporate rates have been reduced to an average of about

---

[173] Daniel J. Mitchell, *"Why Tax Havens are a Blessing"* Foreign Policy, March 18, 2008.

27 percent. It is largely globalization not ideology that has driven this virtuous "race to the bottom." Governments are cutting taxes because they fear that jobs and investments will flee across national borders. Tax havens, by providing a safe refuge for people seeking to dodge confiscatory tax rates, have played a critical role in these positive developments. Better to get some revenue with modest tax rates, lawmakers have concluded, than impose high tax rates and lose out.

Second, European Duchies and Caribbean isles aren't the only places that welcome tax refugees. The United States, for instance does not tax interest and capital gains received by foreigners who invest in America. And since the IRS does not collect data on those payments, there is rarely any information to share with foreign tax collectors. Moreover, U.S. corporate structures, such as Delaware and Nevada companies, are excellent vehicles for foreigners to manage their investments. Thanks in part to these attractive policies; foreigners today have more than $12 trillion invested in the United States. Yet if Merkel's efforts are successful and all nations are saddled with the obligation to help enforce foreign tax laws, it is quite likely that a substantial share of that job-creating capital will flee the United States.

Finally, there is even a moral case for tax havens: They play a critical role in protecting people who are subject to religious, ethnic, sexual, political, or racial persecution. Most of the world's population lives in regimes that have inadequate human-rights protections, and people with assets often are targets of oppressive governments. The ability to put money in a tax haven offers important protections for these potential victims. Even the United Nations, in a 1998 report attacking tax havens, felt compelled to admit that, "For much of the twentieth century, governments around the world spied on their citizens to maintain political control. Political freedom can depend on the ability to hide purely personal information from a government.

Despite the strong arguments for leaving tax havens alone, international bureaucrats see an opportunity to expand their reach. The OECD is seeking to take advantage of the Liechtenstein controversy by rejuvenating its "harmful tax competition" campaign against "uncooperative tax havens" the very countries that help drive better tax policy".[174] Marshall J. Langer, an eminent International Tax scholar affirms by stating that "The United States still does not tax interest on bank deposits of foreigners, nor does it generally require any reporting of these deposits of foreigners, except those paid to Canadian residents. Therefore, it cannot and does not give any information concerning such deposits to any country other than Canada. The United States now also exempts portfolio interest and capital gains, both long-term and short term, other than real estate gains.[175]

As a result of the existence of Tax Havens there is tax competition and a 'race to the bottom' of tax rates. Incidentally OECD has just reported that the weighted average (accounting for country size) corporate rate of non-U.S. OECD nations is now below 30 percent for the first time in history. 2009 marks the 12th consecutive year in which the average corporate tax rate of non-U.S. OECD nations has been below the U.S. rate. With a combined federal and state corporate tax rate of 39.1 percent, the U.S. continues to impose the second-highest

---

[174] Daniel J. Mitchell, *"Why Tax Havens are a Blessing"* Foreign Policy, March 18, 2008

[175] Marshal J. Langer, "Harmful Tax Competition: Who are the real Tax Havens?" Tax Notes International (Special Reports), 18th December, 2000.

overall corporate rate among industrialized countries. Only Japan's 39.5 percent combined rate is higher.[176]

I posit therefore, that Offshore banking in Tax Havens have a 'positive' value to the global financial system. It not only serves the seven vital functions of the global financial system (savings, wealth, liquidity, credit, payment, risk protection and policy) but facilitates 'Tax Competition' which gives Multi-Nationals and Investors the opportunity to compete and maximize their risk return efficiencies. Offshore banking also advances civil liberties in the right to privacy, self preservation, freedom to contract and the right to flee despots into 'Tax Havens'. Recent efforts by OECD and other interest bodies to 'shut down' or isolate and punish offshore financial centers based upon the premise of OFC's complicity to money laundering and terrorist financing lacks currency, hence unfortunate.

---

[176] Scott A. Hodge and Andre Dammert, "U.S Lags while Competitions Accelerate Corporate Income Tax Reform", Fiscal Fact No. 184, Tax Foundation (2009), at *http://www. taxfoundation.org/fiscalfacts*